Refinishing Antique Furniture

Michael Bennett

DRYAD PRESS

1st Edition 1980 © Michael Bennett

ISBN 85219 139 1

Printed in England by David Green Printers Ltd, Kettering
for Reckitt & Colman Leisure Ltd.

My thanks to Claude Lebrun, who taught me most of the techniques described in this book and who read the manuscript for me.

I am also grateful to Del Jones for his enthusiastic support throughout the tedious stages of preparing draft manuscripts and checking proofs.

CONTENTS

PREFACE

I imagine that most of the pieces of antique furniture scattered throughout the homes of this country are in need of some care and attention—a chip of veneer here, a wobbly leg there, amounting to lots of work for the restorer. Many bits of furniture in need of attention must be left to the professional restorer, whose specialist knowledge, equipment and materials enable him to do the most satisfactory and economical job. There are, however, many hundreds of pieces which careful repair in the home workshop can bring back to prime condition.

In this small book I make no attempt to delve into the intricacies of the cabinet-work side of restoration—it's not a subject which can be adequately covered by general rules and to describe by example the many and varied problems which may be encountered would require several volumes. I mention those aspects of cabinet-work which have a direct bearing on the results of finishing and I only deal with those finishing techniques which are likely to be within the scope of the home workshop; techniques which, I should add, are applicable to finishes likely to be found on most English furniture made up to about the middle of the 19th century.

I have described the processes in as near as possible the order in which you might expect to have to do them and I have gone into a fair amount of detail, supporting the text with diagrams and photographs wherever necessary.

Some of the techniques may seem, on first reading, to be hard work. Well, many of them are, but there are no short cuts—no quick and easy methods—in restoration work; not if you want to produce a result which will withstand the test of time.

Michael Bennett
1980

PART I

CABINET-WORK

The size and complexity of the job you can manage in your workshop will not only depend on your skill but also on the range of equipment and materials at your disposal.

Assuming that you have all the necessities for cabinet-work, and the skills required to practise the basic techniques involved, I will start by mentioning one or two points which lead directly into finishing work. If these are not done well, the end result may be a repair which shows, no matter how good the finish you put over it.

All repairs to wood and veneer must be completed before any attempt is made to clean and renew a finish. You will avoid wasting time and effort by sticking to this rule. As with all rules, there is an exception — if you can't be sure what is beneath a layer of stained varnish or heavy grime then you may well have to remove the finish to find out the extent of the repairs required.

1. Identifying woods — Cutting and fitting — Joints

Identification

Recognising the woods you are working on is fundamental to successful finishing: if you cannot identify a wood it will be all the more difficult to match. It is a fairly straightforward matter to learn the features of new wood, particularly if you have the opportunity to handle specimens which demonstrate the varying patterns which different cuts produce. Most of the woods you are likely to come across in English furniture are listed in Appendix A, with a brief description of their characteristics and use in furniture construction and decoration. The problems of recognition really begin when the wood is covered with a finish, the more so when both wood and finish are then mellowed by scores of years of sunlight, polishing and daily use.

Matching woods

Your collection of solid woods and veneers may not be extensive, but do try to match new to original, even though the repair is to a seldom-seen surface.

Three features are most important: colour, graining and figure patterns, and reflectivity.

Colour

Match the colour and shades as closely as possible, but if you can't manage an exact match choose a piece which is paler rather than darker. It's easier to darken a patch than to make it lighter, as you will discover. (Remember that most woods change colour when finished, so check by dampening with a drop of meths.) If you can take a patch from a piece of wood with an aged and mellow surface, so much the better.

Grain and figure

Select a piece with the same general markings of grain and figure lines if possible. The more precisely these match, the easier it will be to disguise the glue-lines round the repair.

Reflectivity

Perhaps the most difficult feature to match is reflectivity, and certainly it's the most difficult to disguise if you do get it wrong. Nearly all woods will appear a different colour and brightness when viewed from various angles, mahogany, satinwood and rosewood being particularly troublesome. The effect has to do with the way in which the fibres lie in relation to the surface, so matching the direction of the grain as viewed from the edges of both the patch and the damaged area will help you to match their reflectivity. In the case of repairs to veneered surfaces this is, of course, far more difficult. In all cases, check and double-check—when you think you have it right, give the piece of wood or veneer from which you are going to cut the patch a wipe of shellac polish (see chapter 6), lay it over the damaged area and view it from all directions, both with and against the light.

8

Always cut patches to follow the lines of grain and figure of the original as closely as possible. In the case of a complex pattern, such as burr walnut, this is easily achieved but where the straighter-grained woods are concerned, one of two shapes is preferable: wedge-shaped for edges (Fig. 1b & d) and boat-shaped for other parts of the surface (Fig. 1a).

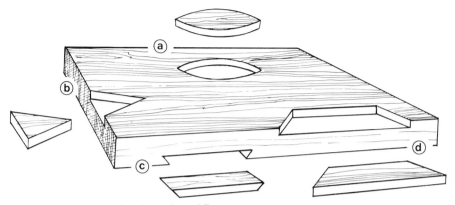

Fig. 1   *Patch in line with the grain and figure*

If a patch in an edge has to take some strain, as for example when reinforcing an area broken away below a hinge, then it should be dovetailed in for extra strength, as shown in Fig. 1c.

Don't try to cut a hole and then fit a patch into it—it will take far too long and the fit is likely to be less than perfect. The procedure I recommend is: Having selected the piece of wood or veneer you want for the repair, draw the appropriate shape on the area to be used for the patch, of sufficient size to cover the damage. Cut out the patch, angling the cut for a boat-shape slightly to give a bevel. Place the patch in position, making sure that it's the right way round—grain, figure, reflectivity remember— and mark round it with a sharp blade (I use a Swann-Morton no. 3 handle with 10A blades). Cut out the damaged or waste wood and try the patch. If your cutting has been accurate, then the patch will fit down to the bottom and right to the edges of the hole. The bevel on the boat-shaped patch will ensure a snug fit at the edges, so reducing the glue-line to the minimum. It is better to err to the inside of the cutting line if you are not sure of getting a perfect fit first time—you can then pare away a little from the hole or patch until it is right. An important point—the patch should ideally end up with its top just proud of the surface (more felt with the fingertip than seen). This is to allow for the effect of the glue, for as it dries it will tend to draw down the patch. Obviously, the judging of the amount to leave proud is not an exact science, so to be on the safe side you will have to leave sufficient to allow for flushing off afterwards. But here we meet another problem: if too much is left proud then the flushing off operation is very likely to reduce the surface to a level where the grain and figure patterns are totally different to the ones you so carefully chose! So, if you are working in solid wood or have used a patching-piece with an old

9

and mellow colour, you can either deepen the hole or take some off the back of the patch, but if it's veneer you only have the latter option. At all costs you must avoid putting in a patch which is going to end up below the surface; it will have to come out in the end because it is sure to show after finishing if not before. If you do happen to flush off to a different configuration, don't worry; whilst it is a shame after the time spent in choosing the patch, it isn't an insurmountable problem, as you will find when you come to disguising the repairs (see chapter 9).

Missing marquetry

Cutting a piece of veneer to replace a missing piece of marquetry is a slightly different problem. First, clean old glue and accumulated wax and grime from the hole. Next, place a piece of plain paper over the hole and rub over briskly and evenly with heelball (melt a little beeswax, add sufficient black pigment to darken it thoroughly, and allow to cool — heelball). The resulting outline can then be traced with carbon paper directly onto the veneer from which the patch is going to be cut, but I find it better to trace it first onto a good-quality tracing paper, through which the details of the veneer can be seen, to aid in the choice of figure and grain direction. Having selected the piece to be cut, then interpose the carbon paper carefully and trace the outline. On simple contours a sharp, pointed blade will do for the cutting, but for complex shapes a piercing saw is best, failing which a fretsaw. (When working with thin or fragile veneer, stick gummed paper behind to support it while it's being cut.) Needless to say, accurate cutting is essential, but if you do wander try to keep to the outer side of the line: you can always trim up when it comes to fitting.

Joints

Another aspect of cabinet-work I should mention concerns joints. Loose and broken mortice and tenon joints will surely be amongst the most common of your problems. Please don't repair them with dowels — apart from not being 'right', they are no long-term answer structurally and cause excessive finishing work. Loose joints must be taken apart as far as possible and have all the old glue cleaned out before regluing; broken joints will require new tenons fitting. Here strength is more important than matching wood so beech is often used, but only when you can work on a concealed surface as for example, on the underside of a chair rail.

2. Gluing—Cramping

Type of glue to use

There are few who will agree as to what sort of glue may or may not be used on antique furniture. To my mind, there can only be one answer— use the glue which the original cabinet-maker used then you can't go wrong.

The only original glue you are likely to find on antique furniture is animal glue, the most widely used today being Scotch glue. Not only is this an excellent adhesive but, unlike many modern glues, it is not irreversible— heat and moisture do affect it. Now this may not seem like an advantage, but when you find you have to open a joint or lift veneer which has been stuck with one of these rock-like (or worse, rubbery) modern adhesives, you'll soon appreciate the point. So only use Scotch glue. Not only will it be compatible (except, of course, with early pegged furniture, which mustn't have glue near it), but you will be doing yourself and any future restorers a favour should the need arise for undoing the work.

The form of Scotch glue which I am accustomed to using comes in small beads, and is called 'pearl' glue. Others are in solid cake form, or liquid.

Preparation of glue

The careful preparation of Scotch glue is important. A couple of handfuls of glue pearls should be put in a shallow plastic container, just covered with cold water and then left to stand for at least two hours, until the water has been absorbed by the pearls. The gluepot should ideally be cleaned out with boiling water between fillings, but so long as the remaining glue is clean and relatively pale you may add to it. Remember though—clean, fresh glue sticks best. (I may be incurring the wrath of some fine old craftsmen by so declaring; some swore that glue should be boiled until almost black.) Use fresh glue and don't let it boil.

Gluepot

As regards the gluepot: an old-fashioned double pot is nice to have, the inner one to contain the glue and the outer one for water. But if you can't get one of those, an old enamelled double boiler will do just as well. The water pot should be three-quarters or so filled and brought to the boil. When it is boiling, reduce the heat to a simmer and fit the glue pot filled with the soaked pearl glue.

Heating glue and checking consistency

The glue must always be thoroughly heated before it's used. You will be able to see when it is getting hot by the wisps of steam which come off when you stir it (after about half an hour). When glue is being freshly made, a scum will form on the surface and this must be removed—try to get it all out in one piece by cutting round the edge and lifting it out with a thin, flat piece of scrap wood. When you think the glue is hot enough to use, test it by brushing a dab across the back of a finger. If it hurts, it's

11

ready! But first, check that it is of the correct consistency for the job by dipping in the glue brush and holding it a few inches above the pot—look at the consistency of the glue as it runs off the brush (Fig. 2). For general work the glue should flow in a steady, creamy stream with no lumps. Too thick and it will have the appearance of hot toffee; too thin and it will break up into thin droplets. When thinning-down glue always use hot water, give it a stir and leave it for a couple of minutes for the temperature to settle. When thickening the glue, add more of the soaked pearls, never unsoaked. For veneering work, particularly where large areas are involved rather than a few small patches, the glue must be of a thinner consistency, but again not so thin that it breaks up when first poured from the brush.

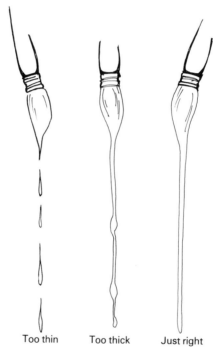

Too thin   Too thick   Just right

Fig. 2   Check the consistency of your glue

Preparing surfaces for gluing

Before gluing, make sure that all surfaces to be glued are free of old glue, wax and dirt. If you don't the fresh glue will be prevented from forming a close, strong bond, resulting in a gap which will not only be unsightly but will cause finishing problems and be a long-term point of weakness. Old animal glue can often be removed fairly easily with a chisel (keep an old one for this purpose) but it will always wash off with hot water; don't use too much water when there is thin veneer about or it may lift, and dry off all surfaces thoroughly as you go along.

New surfaces should be roughened to provide an additional key for the glue. If you don't have a toothing plane, the teeth of your tenon saw will do very well. For small patches, hold the blade of the saw in your vice and draw the patch over the teeth.

It is an advantage to warm all surfaces to be glued just prior to the gluing operation. If this is not always practicable, at least make sure that gluing is done in a warm atmosphere with no draughts. Even with the best of conditions, you will only have a couple of minutes to get the surfaces close up and cramped before the glue starts to form a gel.

Cramping

In this connection, it is essential to have everything ready to secure the joins *before* you start to glue up. It's no use putting glue on a joint then wandering around looking for the right size of cramp! On a complex job it is as well to have a practice without glue, then you will see how the joins are going to react to the various stresses and adjust the layout of cramps accordingly. In all cases, make sure you have the right cramps ready, opened to just over the distance required to go on and, most important, a good supply of cramping blocks (otherwise called 'softening') to hand.

Cramping blocks

Cramping blocks are necessary to avoid marking surfaces. This might seem obvious, but there are enough fine pieces of furniture about with unsightly circular depressions to prove that the word has not yet spread far and wide. Any softwood will do for cramping blocks. They are placed between the jaws of the cramp and the work and must be of sufficient size to spread the pressure evenly over the gluing area. When a block has to be used on a surface on which there is likely to be any trace of glue, the surface of the block which is to be in contact with the work must either be rubbed well with paraffin wax or have one or two thicknesses of newspaper placed between it and the job.

Washing off excess glue

When the join has been satisfactorily glued and cramped, wash off as much of the excess glue as you can with warm water, drying thoroughly with a clean rag as you go along. Don't worry if you cannot get all the glue off at this stage; there's always likely to be somewhere you can't get to—behind cramps usually—but it will wash off quite easily after the join has dried and been uncramped. Obviously, though, it's better to get as much off as possible while it is still relatively soft.

Uncramping

A final word on gluing: Don't be in too much of a hurry to take the cramps off—resist the temptation to "just see how it's going", as it might very well do that. Leave the job overnight at least, particularly in winter. And then when you do remove the cramps, on no account wade straight in to flush off and finish. Let the join settle down for several hours, preferably a day or even more if it's cold and damp, for when the pressure is taken off, the wood is likely to expand and also the glue will still be drying and drawing the surfaces closer together.

3. Sharpening tools

When all your repairs have settled down properly, as described at the end of the previous chapter, any necessary flushing off and trimming can be done. Which brings us to another fundamental of cabinet-work: keep all edge tools very sharp. Blunt tools are not only hard to use, but the very bluntness tends to make you use more force and so cause damage, leading once more to extra finishing work.

Stones

A set of good-quality oilstones and slipstones is essential, in coarse, medium and fine grades. Buy the best you can (or get some good old ones and trim them up yourself, as described at the end of this chapter).

Angles of bevels

When sharpening chisels you are likely to find that a true, sharp edge is easier to achieve and maintain if you grind and hone to *one* bevel instead of the customary separate ground bevel and honed bevel. The angle of the bevel should be between 25° and 30° for firmer and bevel-edged chisels (depending on how well they hold a sharp edge—if they blunt quickly, tend towards a 30° bevel), whilst the harder-working mortice chisels should get 30°. Because of the large area you would otherwise have to hone, plane blades should get the standard double bevel, except for a low-angle end-grain plane, which should be given a single 25° bevel.

Honing

Only occasionally need the coarse oilstone be used, usually when the blade has found a hidden nail and then only when you don't have access to a whetstone on which to regrind the bevel. The medium and fine stones should be used in succession, lubricated with a little thin mineral oil. The procedure for their use which I describe below does without the oft-recommended honing guide—it really is quicker without.

Chisels

To sharpen a chisel, rest the bevel on the oiled stone, checking by feel that it is seated flat—rock it gently back and forth on the back edge of the bevel and you will soon get the feel of when it's flat. Make regular figure-of-eight movements over the whole area of the stone (to keep the wear even) until a burr is felt to be forming on the back face of the chisel (Fig. 3a). Turn this burr with one firm stroke backwards, keeping the back of the chisel *absolutely flat* on the stone (Fig. 3c). A razor edge will be impossible to achieve if the handle is allowed to lift even a fraction. Alternate between figures-of-eight on the bevel and single strokes on the back until all trace of the imperfection has been removed.

Now comes the production of the fine cutting edge. With the bevel flat on the medium stone, give it a half-dozen small circular strokes (Fig. 3b), turn the blade over and give one flat, backward stroke (Fig. 3c). Repeat, with five circles on the bevel and one straight on the back, then four on the bevel and one on the back, and so on down to one on the bevel and a final one on the back. The edge will now be sharp enough for most ordinary work, but if you require a razor edge, as you undoubtedly will for fine trimming, then repeat this routine using the fine stone.

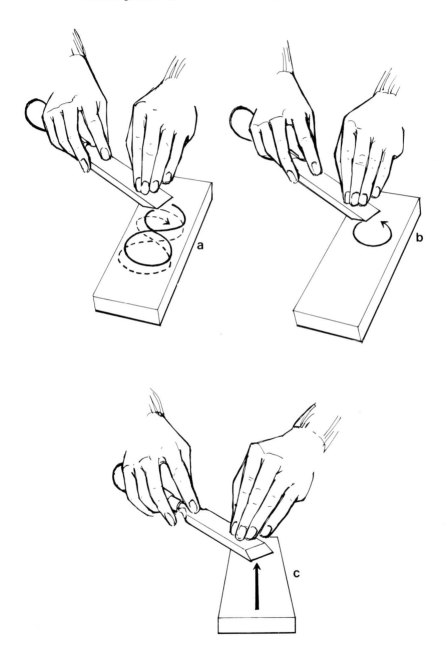

Fig. 3   *Honing a chisel*

Sharpening plane blades follows the same routine as chisels except that the cutting bevel is formed by slightly raising the back of the blade so that only the tip of the ground bevel is resting on the stone. A low-angle end-grain plane blade should be treated exactly as a chisel.

Gouges, of course, are a different problem. Their outer faces, whether bevelled (firmer gouges) or flat (scribing gouges), are treated on oilstones, by rubbing along the length of the stone on an even plane whilst giving a twisting motion to ensure that the whole of the cutting edge is covered. Their inner faces are treated with slipstones, which are rubbed to and fro along the cutting edge.

If your oilstones eventually develop uneven wear they must be trued up, or you will find it impossible to get a straight and true edge to your blades. Truing up a stone is simple but hard work.

Clean off all oil with carbon tetrachloride. Mix some fine silver sand with a little water to a paste on a flat piece of scrap marble or thick glass, then grind the oilstone firmly, with a circular motion, over the whole area. Turn the oilstone round from time to time to ensure that the wear is even. Depending on how severe the damage is, you may need to add more water and sand as you go along. After an hour or so of this—rinse off and leave to dry!

4.   Abrasives

If all has gone well with your job so far, there should be little or no need for the use of abrasive papers. When you do need them, you must avoid the use of coarse-grit papers—they are not necessary and can cause you extra work.

Types of paper
For general cabinet-work two papers are recommended: garnet paper in 150 grit (4/0) and 320 grit (9/0). Garnet paper is more expensive than glass paper but it lasts longer, does not clog easily, and gives a more consistent result.

For finishing work, silicone carbide paper (Lubrisil) in 320 grit is recommended, and it is at that stage of the job where steel wool is used, as described later.

Some general rules for the use of abrasive papers:

Dividing the sheet
Don't use a sheet whole, nor in pieces torn off at random. Divide each sheet into thirds across its width, draw the back surface of the strips to and fro across the edge of your bench to take the stiffness out, then fold each into a three-thickness pad, as shown in Fig. 4.

a

b

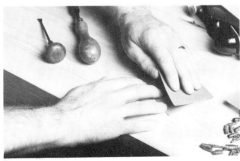

c

Fig. 4   Making a pad of abrasive paper

17

When sanding bare wood always try to keep the movement in the same direction as the grain, not across it. You may not notice cross-grain marks while you are doing the sanding, but when you come to apply the finish they will stand out and ruin the effect. When sanding metal, such as brass inlay, you must keep all the strokes in the same direction; even the slightest mis-stroke will show up, particularly with the finish on top of it.

Unless you are treating an absolutely flat surface (and there are not many of these on antique furniture) don't use a sanding block. The pad of garnet paper held lightly beneath your fingers (Fig. 5) will follow the contours and avoid cutting through high spots.

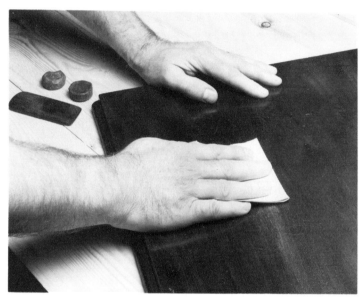

Fig. 5   Holding the pad of abrasive paper

On large areas of new wood, wipe over the surface with a damp cloth after sanding with 150 grit paper. This will raise the grain, which can then be smoothed off with 320 grit paper when the surface has dried. To make sure, do it twice—raising and smoothing the grain a couple of times will prevent problems occurring at the finishing stage, particularly when the surface in question has to be bleached, about which more later.

Finally, don't throw away your used abrasive paper unless it is dirty and crumpled. It will be most useful later on.

And so to finishing . . .

PART II

FINISHING — BASIC TECHNIQUES

The following chapters deal with the finishing processes generally required after repairs to woodwork. When you have mastered these you will be able to tackle the majority of ordinary finishing problems.

Our one objective in applying these processes is to reproduce as closely as possible a surface which has been mellowed in colour over the years and has developed a fine patina. This brings us to a basic rule of finishing: when you have an old, attractive finish, take care to disturb it as little as possible.

Whilst some of the materials used are not chemically identical to those used by the old craftsmen, their effect can be quite as good. The basis of most finishes used on furniture since the 16th century has been varnish in various forms. Varnishes of oil (linseed, poppy, etc.) in which was dissolved a resin such as copal or lac were the first to be used, these being largely superseded by spirit-based varnishes by the early-18th century. The shellac polishes of today are the descendants of those 'shell-lac' varnishes. (French polish does not exist, strictly speaking; french polish*ing* is correctly the term used for the technique of imparting a high gloss with a shellac polish.)

Very early pieces of furniture, and many country-made pieces since, have been treated from new with nothing but wax polish. This finish is described in chapter 15.

Some Victorian (and later) furniture, and some older pieces restored in those times, are to be found finished with a cheap varnish. The signs of this are usually obvious: opaque, pale ochre in colour and often deeply crazed, it conceals most of the detail of the surface beneath. Even when this finish is in reasonable condition, it is not compatible with shellac polish and the only course is to remove it all, as described in chapter 16.

So, on to the finishing routines. As I said before, these are described in roughly the order in which you may have to tackle them, but don't take it as a rigid format to be followed at all times. It is most unlikely that you will be able to predetermine the stages of restoring a finish. You may know what the first step is, and also what you think is likely to follow, but until each step is completed and you can see the result, you will not *know*.

In nine cases out of ten, your piece of furniture will be finished with a shellac which is compatible with a modern spirit-based shellac (albeit with some wax on top — but don't worry about that). Test the finish by dampening a fingertip with meths and rubbing a small, out-of-sight area. As it dries, rub it with a dry fingertip. If it's tacky then you are almost sure to have a surface which will take shellac polish, but the true test will only come when you actually try shellac on it . . .

5. Cleaning and preparing the surface (shellac finishes)

The purpose of the following process is to lift a thin layer of an existing shellac finish, together with any light deposits of grime, in preparation for further finishing. Should you have been fortunate enough to have matched your wood or veneer perfectly for colour, figure, grain and reflectivity, and the repair is in such a place as not to attract the immediate attention of the eye, then it might be all that is required apart from a polish with wax, for this process does tend to move the old finish over a repair and help to blend it in. It is, however, unlikely that you will get away so easily.

Start with a lint-free rag well dampened with meths, wiping evenly over the whole surface, not just the immediate area of the repair. The degree of dampness of the rag is crucial: too much meths and it will lift all the existing finish, too dry and it won't dissolve any, or worse, it will drag and damage the finish. The first application will not necessarily make much impression, but if it is followed straight away with a couple more the finish will usually start to blend and move over the whole surface. Where there are heavy deposits of grime and old wax it may be necessary to apply the meths with steel wool. Use 3/0 grade steel wool, again lightly dampened with the meths, and rub *very* gently. Follow up with a meths-dampened rag to clean up, and don't worry if white streaks appear when the meths dries out; they are easily removed with dry steel wool, this time the finest, 4/0 grade, rubbing gently with the grain.

PLEASE BE CAUTIOUS — AND DON'T OVERCLEAN. Steel wool can rub through to the wood in a jiffy, particularly when used with meths, and can go on through a nicely faded surface to the raw wood below. Don't try to clean all the grime off. Every piece of antique furniture which has been used at all has some grime somewhere, particularly in crevices in carving and turning, and in mouldings. So long as it is not excessive leave it there — it looks all wrong if the piece is so clean that it could have just come from the cabinet-maker's workshop.

6. Shellac polishing

After cleaning and preparing a shellaced surface a few more coats of shellac polish will usually be required to seal it and build it up. In this chapter I will describe the *whole* routine for shellac polishing, although there are several other processes which take their places at various stages of finishing by this method, such as:

Filling blemishes and grain (chapters 7 and 8)
Disguising repairs (chapter 9)
Colouring and staining (chapter 10)

Apart from anything else, it is best to describe this technique here since all the above chapters refer to the use of that essential piece of the restorer's kit — the shellac rubber.

Types of shellac polish

For this process I recommend that you use transparent polish or a very pale button polish. These may be sold under such names as Transparent Polish, Transparent Button Polish, Extra Pale Polish or Special Pale Button Polish. Whatever, the object is to find a polish which is clear and has little or no colour in it, so that the colour of the surface shows through unchanged.

Making a polishing rubber

Shellac polish is most often applied with a rubber, similar, in principle at least, to those you may have seen described for use in french polishing. For this method only one form of rubber is required, consisting of a square of wadding which is folded then wrapped in a square of cloth. For the best results only use the fine wadding obtained from cabinet-makers' suppliers, and only clean, lint-free white cloth such as old sheeting or handkerchief linen.

Experience will show you what size of rubber best suits your hand, but to start with, try this:

Cut a piece of wadding of about 10″ × 10″ and a piece of linen the same size. Fold the wadding into an inverted kite-shape, then knead it to a pointed pear-shape (Fig. 6 a to d). Place the shaped wadding into the linen square, point towards one corner and about 3″ from it, with the open part uppermost. Hold the point between forefinger and thumb with the rest lying on your palm (Fig. 6e). Starting at the point, fold and twist the loose linen to form a rope along the back of the rubber, making sure that you take up all the slack material. A 'tail' will form as you get to the base of the rubber; tuck this up so that it rests comfortably into your palm (Fig. 6 f to k). Make certain that the point of the rubber is maintained throughout this operation — without it you will find it difficult to get polish into corners.

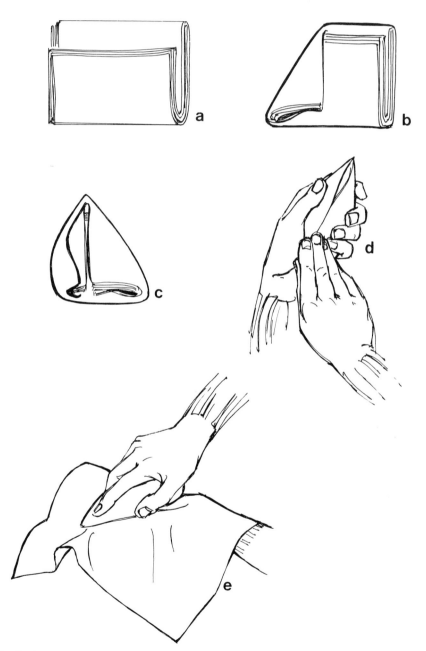

Fig. 6   Making a rubber for shellac polishing

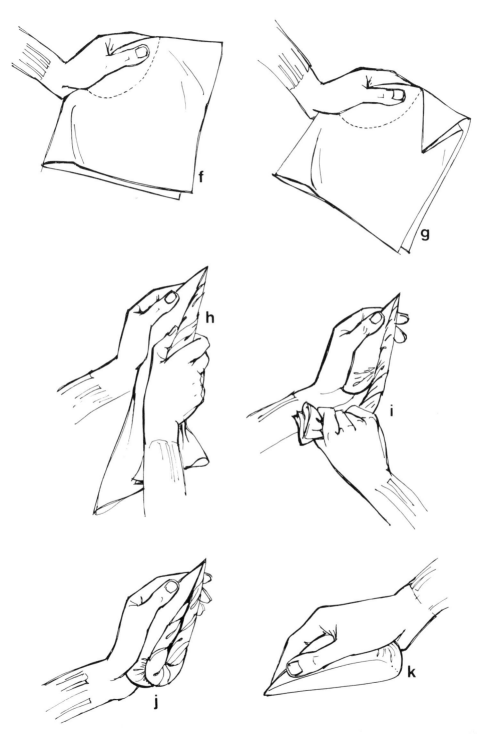

f

g

h

i

j

k

The rubber now has to be charged with shellac polish. I'm sorry but the only way to do this satisfactorily is to undo that carefully twisted linen. Expose the wadding and open it out slightly, then pour in the polish a little at a time and squeeze it in with your thumb, until the wadding is well wetted with polish — but not so that it is dripping out. Remake the rubber and test it by pressing firmly with your thumb. If polish just oozes through the linen that's fine, you are ready to polish. Usually there will be a surplus — too much for proper working — which will drip out when the rubber is pressed. Pat the rubber firmly against a flat surface such as the leg of your work-bench and when you think the surplus has been removed, test again with your thumb. The amount of polish in the rubber for optimum efficiency can only be judged with experience: too much and the surface will show runs of polish; too little and the rubber will drag across the surface without laying down any polish or worse, will pull up previous coats.

Do have some practice on a piece of planed and sanded scrap before you lay into your treasured heirloom.

Before I describe the method of applying shellac polish, there are a couple of tips about storing your polishing rubber, shellac and meths.

Keep your rubber in an airtight plastic container when it's not in use, and it will remain useable for months. Get into the routine of putting it in its box *whenever* you are not actually polishing with it. The only times you will need to make a new rubber will be when the wadding has got so completely compacted that the polish is not being applied evenly and smoothly. When the outside cover gets too dirty, or torn, simply fit a new piece of linen. If you are not using your rubber very often, check it occasionally and if it feels too dry put on a few drops of meths and reseal it in its container.

If your shellac polish has been supplied in a container made of metal, you are advised to decant it into a plastic container once it has been opened or you may find dark spots developing in it, particularly if you are not using much polish and it has to stay in the container a long time. And obviously it is not practicable to be pouring polish or meths from a large container in the small quantities you will actually be using at any one time — keep the quantity of each which you will need for day-to-day use in squeezy-packs, such as the one pint size liquid soap containers. Not only does this facilitate pouring the liquids in controllable quantities, but less damage is done (and loss incurred) when you knock them over. Evaporation from these containers is negligible but you can plug them with a matchstick if you wish.

Shellac polish must be applied in good light, preferably natural light. Try not to work in overhead artificial light as this tends to create deceiving shadows.

The method of applying shellac will vary depending on the existing finish, i.e. a surface which has been fused by the meths treatment described in the previous chapter may only require a few wipes of the rubber, whilst a bare surface will need the full treatment.

On absolutely bare wood, the initial coat of shellac should be applied with a firm, circular motion to ensure that some goes in all the grain to seal it. Subsequent coats used to build up, or 'body up', the surface should be applied with firm but gentle straight strokes over the entire surface, working with the grain, from one end to the other in clean, unbroken sweeps (Fig. 7).

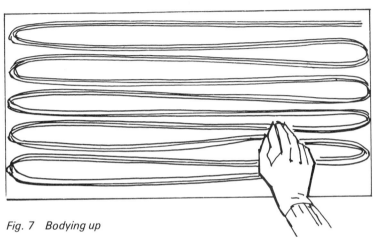

Fig. 7 Bodying up

Time between coats of polish

The time left between coats for the polish to dry will vary depending on the temperature, the humidity, the amount of polish already on the surface, the amount of polish in the rubber, the size of the area being polished and on what operation is being planned next. I think that's all!

Temperature and humidity. Bloom

Ideally a temperature of 65-70°F is best for shellac polishing, with low humidity. If it is cold and damp the polish will certainly go on but it won't dry quickly and you will notice streaks and patches of opaque 'bloom' develop in the polish. If this happens, don't go on polishing: stop until the surface looks completely clear again, indicating that it has dried sufficiently to continue. Bloom can develop in warmer conditions if too much polish is going on, and the same applies—let it dry.

Test for dryness

A test to ensure that the polish is dry enough to go on with another operation, such as staining: pass the back of your hand gently over the surface and if it is felt to drag, and the polish feels cool, it means that all the spirit has not evaporated (feel the difference between a new coat of polish and one an hour old).

Polish in the rubber

The amount of polish in the rubber? Pat the rubber on the palm of your hand from time to time to test the feel—you'll soon get to know if it's charged enough to work properly. When it is too dry it won't run over the surface smoothly and will need recharging—don't use linseed oil, or any other oil recommended for french polishing, in this polishing process.

To top up the rubber, undo it as before, and open up the wadding a little so that the polish goes right inside. Take care to avoid getting strands of wadding stuck to your fingers, as these can easily be transferred to the face of the rubber and then onto the polished surface, with predictable results. You can avoid this problem by dripping the polish onto the outside of the rubber, but this tends to be slower because the rubber cannot absorb the polish quickly and evenly. It's all right, though, when you only require a little polish at a time on the rubber (a fully-loaded rubber can be a disadvantage if you are working on a small area—you are likely to have too much drying time between coats), but when you are polishing a large table top the open method is best. Opening the rubber to charge it also gives you the opportunity to tighten the linen cover, which will slacken as the wadding becomes more compact with use.

*Size of
surface*

When you are polishing a large surface, given that all the above factors are in your favour, you should be able to put on several coats of polish without stopping for anything other than to charge the rubber. If you follow the procedure for application described before—straight strokes from one end to the other—by the time you have completed one coat you can start again at the beginning. After a few coats, and particularly if the rubber begins to drag even though it's properly charged, stop for a few minutes then check the feel of the surface (as described above) before continuing.

Next operation

Then, what operation is being planned next? If you are intending to stain, only one sealing coat is required before the stain is applied, with one or two coats between each application of stain. The same applies for disguising repairs with pigments and stains, although in this case the application of shellac polish is generally limited to the area of the repair. Apart from these sealing and fixing coats, the bodying up of a surface cannot be accomplished in a specified number of coats. It all depends on what it looks like to you—sometimes a half-dozen coats will produce an even surface, but bear in mind the following two points. One—the polishing process is to be followed by matting down with steel wool (as described later) and if there isn't sufficient polish on top of stains and pigments you will cut through them. Two—shellac polish always settles down after a few hours, and what may look like a sheet of glass when you've finished could be showing open grain and unevenness by the following morning. You will then have to either body up with a few more coats of polish or, if you consider that there is enough polish but it is just uneven, you will need to 'pull over' the surface, about which more in a moment.

If, during the bodying up process, or indeed during any operation involving the use of shellac polish, something goes wrong and you have to rub a spot down, do leave it until the surface is completely dry. If you don't you will tear up the polish and leave bits of steel wool or abrasive grit stuck in the soft surface. So leave it for a while and save yourself hours of work.

*Application with
brush or mop*

On carving, close turning, and other areas where the point of your rubber cannot reach, shellac polish can be applied with a sable brush or, on large areas, with a squirrel-hair mop. The polish should be thinned with about

25% meths and the brush or mop thoroughly drained of excess polish to ensure that no runs occur. Don't try to 'work' the polish, just pass the brush once over with a smooth stroke. In fine detail, it will only be necessary to apply one or two coats as it is unlikely to be affected when the higher parts are matted down with steel wool.

When a satisfactory surface has been built up, if it is absolutely even and you are sure that the grain and minor blemishes are filled, leave it overnight to dry out thoroughly. Don't worry about any dust which settles on the surface—it won't do any harm and if you try to brush it off you are likely to make scratches. And don't cover it with a dustsheet or you might find a hairy piece of furniture next day!

Pulling over

If you are not entirely satisfied with the evenness of your finish or if there is likely to be unwanted open grain showing, then, as I said before, you will have to pull it over. This operation should preferably be done the same day as bodying up, within a couple of hours of it and while the shellac is still relatively soft. Often, however, you don't realise that pulling over is required until the next morning, in which case a couple more coats of polish will be necessary to prepare the surface.

The pulling over process sounds a bit drastic but it is in fact quite simple providing a few straightforward rules are followed—and it's very good exercise.

Make sure the surface is free of dust. Pour a few drops of meths onto the rubber (the same one you used to body up, which should be all but exhausted of polish and feel fairly dry to the touch). Starting with small circular movements (Fig. 8a) go over the whole surface, pressing just hard enough for the meths to pick up and move a thin film of shellac, without leaving wet streaks and without dragging. As the rubber dries out, so the pressure must be increased but not to the point of sticking—when it begins to drag (you'll soon get to know the feel of this) add a few more drops of meths to the face of the rubber. Work quickly and get into a rhythm, and don't let the rubber stop on the surface—start and finish each series of strokes with a flourish. Go over a couple of times with circles, and then go to small figure-of-eight movements, the length of the eight along the grain, working across the surface from one side to the other (don't forget to keep the rubber just dampened with meths). The area covered by each band of figures-of-eight will of course depend on the size of the surface. For a surface longer than about three feet the first figures should cover a quarter (Fig. 8b). Then go straight on to larger figures-of-eight, covering a third of the surface, then to cover half the surface, and then all of it (Fig. 8 c to e). Finally, straight strokes with the grain as for bodying up (Fig. 8f). The only pauses in this routine should be to add a few drops of meths to the face of the rubber.

The surface should now have the beginnings of a high, even gloss. I say 'beginnings' because it's most unlikely that one treatment will be sufficient—several, in quick succession, may be necessary. However, you may get to the point where the rubber, in spite of being properly

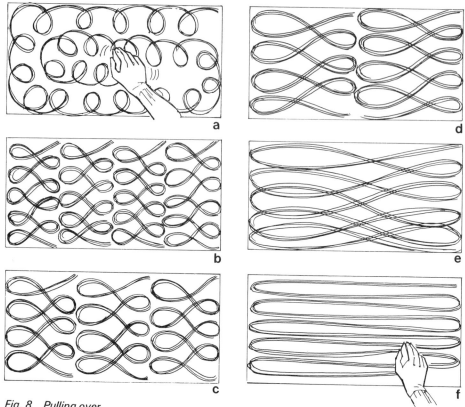

Fig. 8   Pulling over

lubricated with meths, starts to drag. If this happens, stop; you've gone far enough for one session and any more could lead to disaster. Leave it for a few hours, give another couple of coats of shellac polish and repeat the process.

Cutting back

I must stress that the high gloss produced by pulling over is not generally desirable. Few pieces of English antique furniture made before the 19th century had such a finish when new, although many were subsequently french polished to look like this. To produce a mellowed patina which is compatible with a fine piece of furniture it will be necessary to dull down, or cut back, this high gloss and then polish well with wax.

So, after the shellac polished surface has well settled and is perfectly dry—leave it overnight at least, preferably a day or two—the surface should be gently rubbed with fine steel wool (4/0 grade). Don't be mean with the steel wool; use a good fistful made up into a flat pad. Start with small circles and follow with straight strokes with the grain, and keep the 'grain' of the strands in your pad of steel wool in the same direction as the grain of the wood on the straight strokes—this will help to prevent the steel wool rolling in contact with the shellac and ensure the smoothest result. Keep it soft and gentle. You don't want to be bodying up and pulling over again to obliterate scratches, which you can get with the finest steel wool if you are heavy-handed.

The result of accurate cutting back will be a fine, dull shine with no trace of scratching. You are now ready to wax, for which refer to chapter 14.

A final word on shellac polishing: *Use as few coats as you can.* Remember, the only reason you are using shellac is to seal in any colour, etc., and provide a base for wax polish. It is far more authentic to have little shellac and more wax — many of the pieces of furniture which have survived a couple of centuries or more with their original varnish finish will by now have had that varnish worn with constant polishing, and the wax used in the polishing will have built up a patina which no shellac polish, by itself, can imitate.

7. Stopping

Before any finish is applied, inspect all surfaces thoroughly for open grain and blemishes which require filling. Small cracks and holes which are not big enough to warrant cutting patches for may be filled with shellac stopping or wax stopping, depending on their size. Wax stopping is only suitable for fine cracks and for grain filling, about which more in the next chapter.

Shellac stopping

To make shellac stopping you will require some shellac flakes, various colours of dry pigments (see Appendix B)—the umbers, ochres and siennas being the most useful—and some $\frac{1}{4}$-inch square lengths of wood cut from scrap. (I should mention that sticks of shellac stopping can be obtained from cabinet-makers' suppliers, but the range cannot hope to be as wide as that which you can make yourself.)

Preparing shellac stopping

Melt a little shellac (a fat pinch will do for one colour) in a shallow tin on the hotplate, not allowing it to bubble too much. Whilst keeping it liquid, stir in enough of the appropriate pigments to give it the required colour—stir it well to make sure that all the pigment is mixed and doesn't leave any small lumps which will show up when you apply it. When it is thoroughly mixed, tip the can up to one corner or side and scrape the shellac together, remove from the heat and, as it cools, dip in the end of one of the sticks and twist it round to collect a ball of stopping. You can roll the ball of stopping on a clean, flat surface to form a thin cylinder-shape, which will help when it comes to applying it. If you can't get all the stopping out of the tin in one go, put the tin on the heat again and add another layer to the now firm stopping on the stick. Make up a few different colours and shades whilst you're about it.

Applying shellac stopping

To apply shellac stopping you will need a soldering iron, preferably one of the small-tipped electrical ones used for wiring jobs. Select the colour of stopping which is closest to the predominant colour of the wood—sometimes, as for example with rosewood, you may need to use two or three different colours. Melt the stopping into the hole without letting it bubble too much, and build it up so that it is slightly proud of the surface. Flush off the excess stopping with a sharp chisel as soon as it is cool, which will be within a few seconds of applying it, and finish off with a gentle rub with silicone carbide paper. If you have matched the colour well it will be hardly visible, requiring no more than a touch of pigment to disguise it (see chapter 9). If the iron has been too hot or you have left it in contact with the stopping too long, then small bubbles may be exposed when you flush off; these may be filled with more shellac (with a cooler iron) or with wax stopping.

Wax stopping is prepared in the same way as shellac stopping, but using beeswax instead of shellac flakes. (Note the precautions against fire when melting wax—see chapter 14.) When the melted wax and pigments have been thoroughly mixed, turn the mixture out into a shallow mould formed from tinfoil. When it's cool enough to handle—careful, the middle may still be liquid when the outside looks hard—it can be rolled in the palm to form handy-sized lumps. Again, make up a few different colours and shades—it is useful for grain filling as well as stopping.

The application of wax stopping is described in the next chapter.

8. Grain filling and colouring

If all you have needed to do to a finish is clean and revive the shellac polish then there should be no problem with open grain, except of course in any patches or other repairs. However, if you have to strip and bleach a surface (chapters 16 and 17) the grain will usually be open; the amount of old stopping, shellac, etc., removed from the grain will depend on how severe the treatment has to be.

Removing existing grain filling

You may have to remove some existing grain filling such as plaster of paris which has gone white, or perhaps there is an excessive amount of white silica in the grain of a freshly finished surface of Honduras mahogany. Whatever reason, the treatment is to prime the surface with a little stripper (see chapter 16 for the recommended type) and rub briskly along the grain with 3/0 grade steel wool, washing off afterwards with meths on a rag. This treatment cannot, of course, be used on a mellow and faded surface.

Filling grain

The method you use to fill any open grain will depend on two main factors: the size of the area to be filled and the condition of the surface of the wood. As you will have realised by now, the latter is the most important consideration. At the risk of boring you by repeating it: anything which involves abrasives must be used with extreme caution when an old surface of good, natural colour is concerned, so read the following processes with that in mind.

Wax stopping

I will deal first with a simple method for use on small areas, which is particularly useful for filling grain in new wood used for repairs. It has the added advantage of filling any minor cracks in glue-lines. (I know there aren't supposed to be any, but they won't be perfect every time!)

First, seal the surface of the wood with one or two wipes with your shellac rubber (see chapter 6) and allow to dry. Select a piece of wax stopping which matches *either* the colour of the grain in the surface in the immediate vicinity *or,* if there is no distinct grain colour, the predominant colour of the wood. Apply the wax by rubbing well into the grain, evenly over the whole area. Remove as much of the surface wax as possible with a hardwood spatula kept specially for this purpose. Great care must be taken not to let the spatula dig in and mark the surface, and to this end make sure that the corners of the spatula are well rounded off. Remove all remaining traces of surface wax with a well-worn piece of silicone carbide paper, first rubbing over firmly with the *back* of the paper (this softens the wax by friction and it flows into the grain, filling any that has been missed with the lump of wax), then lightly with the face of the paper with a circular motion to remove all traces of surface wax. Finally, seal with a wipe of the shellac rubber.

This process may safely be used on a faded surface if performed with caution, but it would obviously be most tiresome to try to fill the grain of a large area in this way.

Shellac polish On an old and valuable surface, particularly of such woods as rosewood and satinwood, it may be necessary to rely entirely on the shellac polishing process (chapter 6) for grain filling. Repeated cycles of bodying up and cutting back, and then pulling over, might be required before the finish shows no open grain.

Beeswax Another method to be used on nice, old surfaces involves the use of beeswax. This is appropriate to those woods which have a more open grain, such as oak and ash, and is ideal for those pieces of furniture which have had little or no shellac varnish (or similar) used for their original finish. The procedure is described in chapter 15.

Pumice Another method I should mention employs pumice to fill the grain. It is intended primarily for filling grain in new wood, and as such was used as the basis for french polishing before plaster of paris and other cheap means of filling came on the scene. I include it here for completeness — precede the shellac polishing routine in chapter 6 with this process and you have the closest thing to french polishing and, who knows, one day you *might* want to try it. But *please* don't use it on a piece of furniture on which it could never have been the original finish.

So, grain filling with pumice: Make up a new rubber with a cover of strong, fairly coarse linen and charge it with meths only, squeezing out the surplus to leave the rubber just damp — there must be no trace of wetness. Sprinkle a little pumice on the surface of the wood. Use a fine-meshed shaker and put on too little rather than too much — the pumice must not be allowed to build up on the rubber or it will destroy the surface it is supposed to be creating. Put two or three drops of shellac polish — no more — on the face of the rubber and rub gently over the whole surface with small circular sweeps, until all the pumice has gone. Sprinkle on another small amount of pumice and continue. If the rubber begins to drag, dampen it with a little more meths and, on a large surface, it may be necessary to put on a drop or two more polish eventually, but only if the pumice appears not to be binding and staying in the grain. Continue with this process until the grain is filled, then clean off any surplus pumice from the rubber, charge it with shellac polish and a squirt of meths, and go over the surface with the same small circles until a shine begins to develop, finishing off with strokes with the grain. Finally, charge your polishing rubber with a 50/50 mixture of shellac polish and meths and start to body up; as you progress, recharge the rubber with polish with less and less meths added, until you are using all polish. Proceed as described in chapter 6.

9. Disguising repairs

A patch inserted into a surface will have a glue-line round it, no matter how accurate your cutting and fitting. In the majority of cases this line will detract from the appearance of the piece of furniture, even though the wood may have been perfectly matched in every way: colour, grain, figure and reflectivity. However, unless your stock of woods is large and extremely varied, it is likely that one or more of these is also less than perfect, so some art-work will have to be done to disguise the repair. An exception to this is furniture which has not, nor ever has had, a shellac or varnish finish, such as medieval oak furniture, on which a patch or repair may reasonably be left to show.

Colours in the wood

Every wood, no matter how plain it appears at first glance, is made up of many different colours and shades, all jumbled together. The overall appearance of a surface might be reddish-brown (warm) but close inspection can reveal flecks of greenish-grey (cool). The reproduction of the colours and patterns surrounding a repair, into and through the repair itself, calls for patient, careful brushwork and a good eye for colour.

I recommend that you do any necessary disguising before any staining is carried out—the overall colouring is a further help in disguising the repair. This work must be done in natural light; not bright sunlight, but good daylight free from reflections. If you attempt to use any colouring medium in artificial light you will most likely find it looks completely different when you come to inspect it in daylight—a patch which has seemed to disappear in the lamp-lit evening can stand out horribly in next morning's light.

Now to what you will need for this process.

Pigments

First: pigments. Dry pigments, also referred to as earth pigments since they are nearly all produced from rocks and minerals, are opaque, non-soluble, fine powders which are colour-fast. A list of the most useful is given in Appendix B. Keep your range of pigments in clear jars so that you can spot the colours you want without having to peer inside or read the labels.

Brushes

Second: brushes. Keep a range of good-quality sable brushes (say sizes 0, 2, 6 and 8) specially for use with shellac-based processes such as this. If you can get them with different coloured handles to those you will require for water stain (see next chapter), so much the better. As with all brushes keep them clean during and after use. Give a good rinse in meths, shake dry, bring to a fine point and stand in a rack (easily made by drilling holes of the appropriate sizes in a block of wood). Don't leave brushes standing in meths, or anything else for that matter, or their tips may bend beyond recovery.

Prepare yourself properly before you start. Carefully inspect the surface you are treating, analyse the colours and get out the appropriate pigments.

Cornet
You will remember I suggested earlier that you should keep your used pads of abrasive paper. This is where they are useful. Tear a pad at its two folds, fold one of the resulting (near) squares into quarters with the abrasive outside and open it out to form a small cornet, which is then a disposable vessel in which to mix pigments (Fig. 9). Ensure that there is a clean edge on which to drain excess mixture from your brush; a torn edge will have loose fibres of paper which may be transferred to the job.

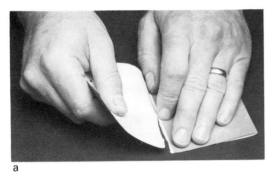

a

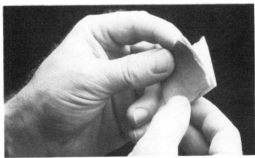

b

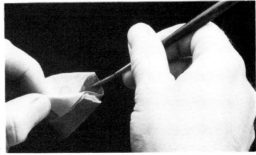

Fig. 9   Making a cornet for mixing colours

c

Get out your brushes, shellac polish and meths containers, polishing rubber and a small jar for meths to wash out the brushes. An eggcup, or anything similar with a diameter of 1½"-2", is useful to stand your pigment cornet in when you're not using it.

Mixing pigments

To begin, put a few drops of shellac polish in the cornet with an equal quantity of meths (the thinner shellacs will require less). Identify the palest and coolest colour in the surface surrounding the repair. Dampen a brush (no. 2 for average-sized work) with the polish mixture, remove the excess on the side of the cornet, and dip the brush into the pigment which appears to be nearest to the colour you have identified. Mix it on the side of the cornet and check it against the job. Too light; too dark? Adjust it with a dip more pigment (the same, or a different one? I said you needed good colour sense!). When it looks right, test it on the surface, but not necessarily on the repair, and adjust the colour until it blends in perfectly with that basic colour you are aiming for. When you are satisfied with the colour, make sure that the addition of pigments hasn't thickened the mixture up too much. You *must* work with a thin mixture — it is tempting when you have found the right match to lay in and try to cover the glue-line with one or two coats, but resist it, for the result will be a lump of pigment which will show up no matter what you put over it. So add more meths and polish if you even suspect that it might be too thick.

Application of pigments

Then, with small strokes (within the size of the flecks of colour in the wood wherever possible), apply the pigment mixture from the centre of the repair outwards along the direction of the figure/grain, following the pale areas through the glue-line (Fig. 10d).

As you progress you will gradually obliterate the glue-line. As the picture builds up, start to warm up your colour to match the other colours on the wood and extend the figure and grain lines over the edges of the repair, and through it if necessary (Fig. 10e).

Don't keep applying pigments continuously to the same spot — between each group of strokes and each change of colour allow a few minutes for the layers to dry, to the point where you can rub your fingers over without feeling a dragging surface. (Rinse your brush in meths at each pause.) It is as well at these stages to give the surface of the pigments a brisk but gentle rub with dry fingers to remove any slight grittiness. Then give the area a wipe with the shellac rubber, which will show the colours truly.

Reflectivity

A most important point: Don't apply pigments whilst facing the work from the same direction all the time. It's our old enemy Reflectivity again — if you don't look at a surface from all angles whilst you are applying pigments and adjust the colours accordingly (small flecks of colour to look right from each direction), you will end up with a patch which may be totally invisible from one direction, but from another stands out like a beacon.

Fig. 10 Stages in disguising a repair
A late-18th century decanter case; mahogany veneer on pine with apple-wood stringing.

10a. The case before restoration. The mahogany veneer has been damaged by screws holding the lock, and there are several pieces of stringing missing.

10b. A close-up of the damaged veneer. The following three pages show stages in repairing this damage.

10c. The main damage has been patched with old mahogany veneer, while the small holes to the right of the keyhole have been filled with hard stopping.

10d. Pale pigments, matched to the palest colour discernible in the surrounding veneer, are used to disguise the outline of the patch and unwanted features.

10e. Colours are developed with warmer shades of pigments to blend the features of the patch with its surroundings.

10f. Graining and other surface features are added with vandyke and water stains.

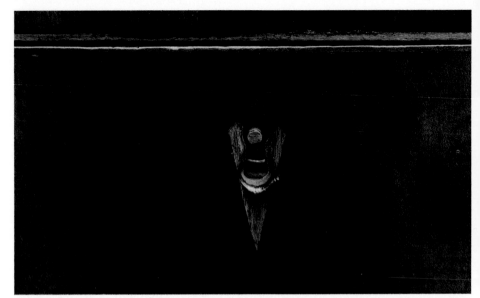

10g. Water stain is applied to match the discolouration round the keyhole. When all repairs and colouring are completed, the repaired areas are given several coats of shellac with a polishing rubber. After drying overnight the shellac is cut back with fine steel wool, and an overall application of wax polish restores the patina.

10h. The job completed. Major damage has been repaired, whilst leaving those marks and stains which give the piece character.

There is no set number of stages through which you will have to go from cool light to warm dark colours. However, beware a large build-up of pigments. If you have a noticeable ridge of pigments you will have trouble disguising it when it comes to bodying up the shellac surface. If this is the case you will have to remove that attempt—wait until it is completely dry and then rub gently with silicone carbide paper (320 grit) or 4/0 grade steel wool, being careful not to overlap the edge of the pigmented area and remove any faded surface beneath.

It may at first take several attempts for you to achieve the correct colouration with a series of thin layers of pigment. When you are satisfied, a final couple of wipes with the shellac rubber will seal it and indicate the next stage, i.e. whether to body up or to add general colouring in the form of overall staining.

Staining Note also that the final stages of disguising a repair are best done with stains (preferably water stains and/or vandyke, as described in the next chapter) rather than pigments (see Fig. 10g). This not only helps to keep the thickness down, but disguises the pigments themselves, the opacity of which tends to be rather prominent unless a transparent colour is on top.

10.   Colouring and staining

Some degree of colouring and shading will usually be necessary on all jobs. There are many materials and methods available to carry out these processes, some of which are downright dangerous—I will describe those which involve least risk (to person or furniture) and are within the scope of the home workshop.

A.   Water stains

These come in a variety of colours in powder form (see Appendix B) and are mixed, of course, with water. Store the powders in well-sealed jars.

Mixing water stain

I find it best to mix a fresh batch for each job as the consistency required is bound to vary; some will require a deep shade or a thicker mixture whilst others will only need a lighter, thinner stain. Experience will show you how much to use, but start with a few drops of water in a shallow dish and add a few grains of powder from the tip of a dry pallet knife—you can always add more powder or water as you go along.

Applying water stain

The stains may be applied with a brush for small areas (keep a set specially for water stains—say sizes 0, 2 and 6 in sable) or with a clean white rag for large areas. Whichever method is used, always work with the direction of grain and figure in order to avoid streaks showing against their pattern.

As a general rule, don't put water stain directly onto bare wood. Apart from the possibility of raising the grain, you will have little control over the effect of the stain; once it is absorbed into the wood you'll have a difficult time if you find it's not the right colour or shade. So, fix the bare surface first with one or two wipes with the shellac rubber, then if the colour isn't right a wipe over with a damp cloth will take you back to start again with no trouble. When the colour is satisfactory and the stain is absolutely dry, fix it with a coat of shellac polish, using the rubber with light, even strokes along the grain. If you don't let it dry completely you will find the shellac you put on top will lift it off, or the surface may craze, which is not often a desirable effect—if the latter does happen, it can usually be rectified with a few coats more of shellac, although this may not be desirable either, apart from delaying you while it dries.

Another don't: Don't try to achieve a perfect match with one application. A few thin applications, fixed with shellac between each, will enable you to build up the colour gradually and controllably.

Finally—those brushes. Don't forget to rinse them well with water after you have used them, bring them to a fine point and stand them in a rack.

B. Vandyke

Whilst this is in effect a water stain, it does deserve special and separate mention. Apart from the fact that its preparation is different to ordinary water stain, its characteristics are such that it might fairly be described as the antique furniture finisher's best friend.

Originally, vandyke was produced by extracting the coloured pigment from walnut husks, which was then dehydrated to form chunky 'crystals'. Vandyke crystals are not generally available now (if you know where they can be obtained I will be most grateful to be told); usually the word 'substitute' follows the name. Even so, vandyke substitute makes a most versatile stain.

Preparing vandyke

Quarter fill a large, flat tin (a 2oz. tobacco tin is ideal, and will contain enough to last some time) with hot water and put it on the hotplate to keep warm. Add vandyke powder to the warm water a little at a time, say a teaspoonful, and stir until dissolved. Go on adding vandyke until it becomes almost impossible to dissolve it, then work this stiff paste until you have an even consistency. Smooth the paste down into the tin with a pallet knife, allow it to cool until it is solid, and it's ready for use.

Applying vandyke

Vandyke may be used for general colouring, for shading to reproduce the natural accumulations which appear in grain, cracks and depressions, inside carving or on much-handled parts of furniture, and for reproducing graining on repaired surfaces. As with water stain, it should not be used on bare wood.

Overall colouring of large areas

To colour large areas, pour a few drops of water into the vandyke tin and mix it thoroughly with a brush—a 1″ paint brush is ideal. Work the mixture about until it is the consistency of thin cream.

Prepare a clean, white rag in the form of a rubber—not exactly as a polishing rubber, but so that there are no lumps and no loose threads trailing. Have another piece of clean rag handy.

Make sure the surface of the wood is fixed with one or two wipes of the shellac rubber. When it is completely dry, apply the vandyke mixture with the brush and then distribute it evenly with the rag rubber. You will have to work quickly as the object is to get an even coat over the whole surface before the water evaporates, which it does surprisingly rapidly. Work with smooth strokes with the pattern of grain and figure, wiping the face of the rag rubber on the other piece of rag if an accumulation of vandyke develops on it. It may be necessary to turn the face of the rubber to a clean area if it gets too wet and sticky.

A word of caution: vandyke is slightly abrasive, so if you rub too hard you are likely to break through the shellac and either force dark streaks into the wood if it's the first application, or smear previous coats of vandyke or other stain. Don't let this statement make you over-cautious— just remember that quick, light strokes are required.

When the vandyke is dry, give it a gentle rub with your fingertips to make sure that no gritty particles are left on the surface. Needless to say, your fingers must be completely dry.

If you are satisfied that the colour has gone on evenly, and that there are no cross-grain streaks, then fix it with a couple of wipes with the shellac rubber.

Shading and reproducing grime

In keeping with the principle of not overcleaning, of not removing *all* the grime accumulated through years of use, so grime has to be put back if a repair has had to be done to an area which carries such an accumulation. In nearly all cases vandyke will accomplish this.

On flat surfaces a heavy consistency of vandyke will be required. Get the vandyke brush almost dry, touch it onto the stiff vandyke mixture in the tin and then dab it onto the appropriate part of the surface. Now comes the important part—with the edge of your outstretched hand, dab the patch of vandyke with a rapid but light chopping action, starting at the centre of the patch and moving it gradually outwards in as random a way as possible, until the vandyke begins to dry out. If you have done it properly the result will be a smudge of grime which might have been there for centuries! Don't be tempted to add some more to the same spot if it doesn't look dark enough—you will only smear the first application. Wait until it's dry, then fix it with a coat of shellac. You will then (and only then) see the true effect of the vandyke, and can decide whether or not more is required.

If you have to shade inside some carving, turning or moulding, apply a coat of vandyke (thick mix) then immediately wipe it off the highlights with a slightly damp rag. When the vandyke is dry further shading-off can be achieved by rubbing over gently with a soft, dry rag. Fix the shading with shellac, using a soft brush or mop charged with a 50/50 mixture of polish and meths.

Graining

A thin mix of vandyke, applied with a fine brush, will nearly always be right to imitate dark graining. If the colour is not quite matched, the vandyke may be adjusted with a little water stain. Graining is usually necessary where a repair has been disguised with pigments (as described in chapter 9), which will have obliterated existing grain (see Fig. 10f).

C. Oil stains

There should not be any need for you to use these. Apart from the fact that they need to be left to dry for several times longer than water stains before they are fixed with shellac, there is not the same control of colour and shade, which is often so critical. If you have to use oil stain, apply it with a fresh piece of muttoncloth, made up into a pad as for water staining, and again remember to work with the grain.

D. Spirit stains

These should not be relied upon to give basic colour to wood because, being spirit soluble, they are likely to be removed or smeared by the shellac rubber. They have their place when it comes to adding a hint of transparent colour (perhaps also with a few grains of earth pigment) when you need to match some colouring which is present in an original finish, or when disguising a repair to a highly-reflective wood.

Spirit dyes are supplied in powder form and are best applied thinly in a 50/50 mixture of shellac polish and meths, using a fine brush or mop. When fixing, use light wipes of the rubber to start with, to avoid spreading the stain too far.

E. Chemical staining

Potassium bichromate

Potassium bichromate is useful for darkening and mellowing a surface to reproduce the effect of natural aging (particularly when the wood is to be left unpolished, as in the case of backs and interiors of furniture — see chapter 12).

Potassium bichromate is supplied in the form of fine crystals which are bright orange in colour. Mix these with cold water to make a saturated solution (i.e. add crystals until no more will dissolve, then put in another few spoonfuls — about $\frac{2}{3}$ water and $\frac{1}{3}$ crystals will do).

Wear rubber gloves when handling crystals and stain. Not only will this chemical discolour your fingers quickly and thoroughly, but it is regarded as a poison.

Application of the stain should be to clean bare wood, using clean rag on large areas, or a piece of scrap wood or a fine nylon brush for small patches. It goes on bright orange but browns as it dries — this colour can be controlled by washing off with water when the right shade has developed. Different woods will show different responses, so always experiment on a piece of planed and sanded wood of the same sort before using it on your repair.

11. Blemishes as features

Distressing Any bit of furniture which has been in day-to-day use has some dents and scratches in and under the finish, which show as dark marks and depressions. Unless they are too prominent, these give a bit of character to the piece. Now, if you have to put a new piece of wood into an old surface, all the features of that surface have to be matched, including dents and scratches, and this is accomplished by the fearsome-sounding technique of 'distressing'. The whole art of distressing is to damage the surface in a completely random pattern with various unscientific devices. It really is more difficult than it sounds, for it's no use being persuaded that the answer lies in taking a length of chain and flailing away in a random fashion — the distribution of the marks may be uneven if you're lucky, but the marks themselves will be nearly all the same shape. I won't go so far as to say that every mark must be individually applied with a different implement, but if you have the patience this will give the best result. Anything that will make a mark can be pressed into service, but use each one only a few times, on different areas and vary the angle and force of each impact. I use a flint nodule which has lots of small, smoothed-off irregularities. This can be rolled, tapped or drawn across the surface to create an extremely varied pattern of marks. For areas which require lots of small, irregular dents the use of a single implement would be too time consuming — try some smooth gravel pebbles in a plastic bag (you'll have to have a number of bags and use each one only a few times, that is unless you don't mind sweeping up the gravel every time a bag bursts).

I must emphasise that the distressing must be done right first time — unlike nearly all the other techniques in this book, which can be rectified fairly easily if something goes wrong, poor distressing will mar the job and be difficult to rectify without replacing the wood.

Use on shellac finishes When to do the distressing? Usually the best stage is after the colouring and shading have been finished and fixed with several coats of shellac (on shellaced finishes only, of course; wax-only finishes are mentioned at the end of the chapter). If you do it any earlier then the dents may be filled with an unnatural colour or too much shellac. When you have completed the distressing to your satisfaction you can fix it with shellac if the dents are to be left clean, which is unusual to see except for the shallowest of depressions. More often there is some degree of shading in the dents for which vandyke is the natural choice to reproduce. Rub the vandyke brush over and into the marks, using a fairly thick mixture. When it is dry, go over gently with silicone carbide paper, held as flat as possible to the surface. Only use sufficient pressure to cut through the vandyke without affecting the layers beneath. When this is done, vandyke will be in the blemishes only and you can then fix and body up as required.

If you have to distress a repair to a piece of furniture which has a wax-only finish (see chapter 15) then it must be done before any wax is applied to the surface. The surface should be fixed with one coat of shellac polish, distressed, have vandyke applied and cut back as described above, then waxed as normal.

12. Unpolished surfaces

Natural
dry surfaces

Preparation
of water wax

Application
of water wax

Quite often it is necessary to repair areas which include unpolished or 'dry' surfaces. Obviously these cannot be finished with shellac or polishing wax, but they must be treated to blend in with their surroundings.

Most inside and concealed surfaces of furniture have a powdery, dry appearance which is best reproduced by the application of a concoction called water wax, which is made as follows:

Melt a small piece of carnauba wax in a very large tin (to hold at least ten times the amount of wax you are melting). This may sound odd but it's important, as you will see.

In a separate tin, heat up the same volume of liquid soap (Teepol) as the wax you are melting. Get both soap and wax hot (do not leave unattended, there is always the danger of fire when melting wax), and when the soap is on the point of bubbling over, and not before, remove both from the heat and start to add the soap in *small quantities* to the liquid wax, stirring well as you do so. Do this very carefully as there is quite a reaction between the two liquids, hence the need for the oversize tin. Continue stirring until the liquids have mixed and started to solidify into a thick paste, then leave to cool and dry out completely.

The resulting water wax will be a light sage-green when unpurified carnauba wax is used. Earth pigments (see Appendix B) are added to obtain the colour required.

Break out some pieces of water wax from the tin and crush them to a fairly fine powder (pestle and mortar are ideal but a block of scrap wood and a piece of board will do nicely). Add to this powder a small amount of each pigment necessary to match the basic colour of the surface. If you get the mix too dark, don't try to lighten it with more pigment or you may end up with a mixture which doesn't adhere to the surface when it has dried out. The only answer is to scrap that lot of materials and start with more crushed wax. When you have the dry colours mixed to the correct tone, put them in a shallow dish and mix with a few drops of water to produce a thin paste. Apply the paste with an ordinary paint brush. Several thin coats, with plenty of drying time in between, are better than one thick one, so avoid the temptation to try to get it done too quickly — it will only have to come off again if you rush it.

When the wax is completely dry, rub over the surface very lightly with 3/0 grade steel wool to level it, after which shading and graining may be put on with vandyke — use the brush almost dry and stipple the surface for shading or flick it along the surface to reproduce graining. With a dry, soft brush, dust on dry earth pigments to give any necessary variations to the colour and texture of the surface, and follow this with an overall dusting with old dust (try the loft, there's bound to be some good old filth up there, failing which, wood ash is a reasonable substitute). After a day or so, give it a gentle rub over with a soft rag to remove surplus pigments and dust, and you should have the appearance of an untouched old surface.

Painted dry surfaces

Many pieces of 19th century furniture, such as chests of drawers and bureaux, are likely to have their backs and undersides coated in a painted-on matt finish, often of a reddish-brown colour, and many pieces which were restored in those times received the same treatment.

When you have to repair such a piece it is best to renew this finish rather than attempt to strip it off and give it an 'older' one. The method is simple, if smelly.

To a teaspoonful of whiting add a half-teaspoonful of each of the appropriate earth pigments and mix together. Add a couple of dollops of Scotch glue from your pot (or cut out a half square inch if it isn't melted, but don't use unsoaked glue) and a couple of fluid ounces of hot water. Mix this pungent goo to a thin wash and apply with an ordinary paint brush. If a bit of variation is required in the tone, a few random dabs with the vandyke brush before the wash is applied will usually give the desired effect.

This finish *must not* be used on a surface which has not had a previous painted finish—bare wood must be treated with water wax or be chemically stained, as described before.

13.　Treatment for woodworm

Woodworm, or more correctly, furniture beetle (even more correctly, the *larva* of the furniture beetle) causes an unnecessary amount of damage to furniture. Unnecessary because, not only can it be prevented, or stopped at an early stage, but also because it seems to cause so much panic when discovered that a piece might be burned "to stop it spreading to the rest of the furniture". Few people realise that by the time they find the first flight holes ("worm-holes"—but actually the holes are made by the newly-hatched beetles breaking through to the outside world), the little horrors have been gnawing away for at least a couple of years, maybe as many as five.

So don't panic when you find a hole. First, check to see if it's old or new: new holes always show clean, fresh timber inside them, and there will be a fine, gritty powder (frass) in evidence on the surface or beneath the site of recent activity. Look out too for the beetles. They are small, averaging under ¼", with comparatively thin brownish-black bodies, and they are most commonly found in mid-summer although any really warm spell will tend to bring them out.

There are two courses of treatment: one, to inject the holes with one of the proprietary insecticides such as those made by Rentokil or Cuprinol or, two, to have the whole piece of furniture fumigated.

Injection Use one of the purpose-made injectors, such as the one produced by Rentokil, which ensure that a good pressure is behind the insecticide to get it into all the galleries. Inject into all the holes you can find, old as well as fresh, to be on the safe side. And don't give just a little squirt into each—keep on until the fluid can be seen tracking along the galleries beneath the surface. A note of warning: don't squeeze the injector vigorously as soon as you've located the pressure nozzle in a hole. A gentle, exploratory squeeze will avoid a fountain of fluid gushing from other holes many inches away from the one you are treating. (Take the precautions recommended by the manufacturer—gloves and goggles will prevent some unpleasant mishaps.)

Whilst you are about the business of injecting the flight holes, give a squirt of the insecticide into any dry, dusty cracks there are, as these are just the places which the beetles are likely to select to lay more eggs.

Fumigation When a piece of furniture is severely infested, if it is of a pale wood which will be stained by liquid insecticide, or if it has upholstery which would be costly to remove and replace, then fumigation by a specialist is the only answer. Also, it is the only course to take if there are holes in a surface which needs refinishing: you cannot allow the oily insecticide on the surface wood, for the finish would not adhere, and of course you can't inject once the finish is on—so get the piece fumigated before you set to work on it.

Prevention being better than cure, you will be wise to look over all undersides and backs of your furniture at least once a year, in early summer, and give all vulnerable areas a squirt with the applicator, rubbing any excess fluid over the surrounding surfaces. This applies particularly to unpolished surfaces—polished surfaces are less likely to be attacked, particularly if kept clean and well waxed.

Finally, remember never to treat with insecticide if you are planning to do any repairs to the woodwork or any refinishing—leave it until afterwards or get the piece fumigated. And don't stop checking after you've had a piece fumigated; whilst most fumigation is guaranteed against new woodworm activity for a number of years, it will not prevent reinfestation for ever.

14. Cleaning and polishing

Washing
Most light films of dirt and grime, whether on shellac or wax finishes, will respond to a gentle wash with kitchen soap and warm water. Obviously the water must not be applied too liberally, nor must too large an area be washed without rinsing and drying. Do a small area at a time, and do make sure that it is dried thoroughly but gently with a soft cloth.

When completely dry, all that should be necessary is a buffing with muttoncloth or, if too dull, a waxing with a good polish, for which I'll give you a recipe in a moment.

Revivers
First, though, a word about revivers. There must be dozens of concoctions which have been devised for cleaning and reviving finishes but, unfortunately, at best they are likely to be only temporarily effective. Some are excellent cleaning agents, particularly those which contain a high proportion of solvents such as methylated spirit or turpentine, but none can produce a good shine as well as can a hard-wax polish. And if the finish is damaged, no amount of reviver or "scratch remover" will solve the problem—you will have to employ the refinishing techniques described in chapters 5 and 6.

Wax polish
Now, wax polish. There are several brands of polish sold nowadays, many of them excellent products based on old, well-tried recipes. However, they all have a major drawback—they are made to be applied easily and therefore cannot contain a high proportion of the hard wax necessary to produce a quick but lasting shine.

Making wax polish
The polishing wax I am about to describe has a high proportion of hard wax, which does make it more difficult to use than the commercial products, but you may be sure that the result is worth the effort.

The recipe is:

Carnauba wax	:	2 parts
Paraffin wax	:	2 parts
Beeswax	:	1 part
Pure turpentine	:	10 parts

} by volume

Dark polish
If you are using unpurified carnauba wax (a dark grey-green colour) and yellow beeswax, the resulting polish will be a dark olive colour, which is fine for most work. If you wish to produce a darker wax, add a tin of dark brown or black shoe polish to the above list.

White polish
If you want a white polish, it will be necessary to use purified carnauba wax (which is not generally available) and bleached beeswax.

To prepare the polish: Melt the waxes in a graduated pan, if you can get one, or mark off the appropriate levels inside a tin. Use a thermostatically controlled electric hotplate, not a naked flame, as there is a high risk of fire; only have the heat setting sufficient to melt the waxes without them smoking or boiling, and keep an eye on the process the whole time. Start with the carnauba wax, melting sufficient to bring the level to its mark, then paraffin wax followed by beeswax and any colouring. The proportions don't have to be *exactly* as the recipe, so it won't matter too much if you go over a mark here or there. It is important to leave enough room for the turpentine — no more than a third of the pan or tin must be filled with melted wax, preferably a lot less to allow for stirring.

When all the waxes have been melted and blended, remove from the heat and immediately stir in the turpentine, then decant into a suitable container (not right to the top, leave at least half an inch). I keep old coffee tins with snap-on plastic lids for this purpose, but any round tin of up to about 5″ depth is suitable so long as there is some way to seal it when not in use to prevent the turpentine evaporating too quickly.

When the polish is cool it will still be too hard to use, in spite of the large amount of turpentine in the recipe. Don't be tempted to melt it down and add more turpentine; you'll certainly make it softer, but no use for the method of application which follows.

Preparing wax polish for application

You will need a good 2″ paint brush with soft but springy bristles, which should be cut down to a tapering ¾″ to 1″. This is used both to mix the wax up and to apply it.

Pour a few drops (no more than a teaspoonful) of turpentine onto the surface of the wax in the tin and mix it up well with the brush. Now, if you haven't left that half-inch I mentioned, there's a fair chance more wax will end up on you than on the job, because this really has to be a vigorous operation. *All* the turpentine has to be mixed in with the top layer of wax. When you think it is all mixed in, scrape the brush out on the edge of the tin, put all the resulting soft wax back into the middle, and give it another go. And then another. After that, the soft wax should have the even consistency of butter in summer. When it has, wipe and squeeze out the brush with a rag to make absolutely sure there's no turpentine left in it. If you don't you may find that the first time the brush goes on the surface it has exactly the opposite effect to that intended — the unmixed turpentine will dissolve any polish already there instead of laying down a fresh coat.

Once you have done this mixing operation you will understand the need for moderation in pouring in the turpentine. If you do put in too much, pour some off rather than try to mix it in or you'll be stirring all day to get the right consistency. On the other hand, don't be so mean with the turpentine that you end up with a crumbly, almost dry, mixture on your brush — it won't spread properly, and if you do succeed in buffing it the result will be streaky.

To apply the polish: Take up a small amount of the softened wax with the brush and rub it over a small area with a circular motion — do no more than a couple of square feet at a time or you may find it too hard to work when you come to the next operations. With a clean, soft rag, immediately remove excess wax from the surface, turning the rag to a fresh area frequently. Don't try to produce a shine, just rub over gently after the excess wax is off, to make sure it's level. Go over all the surface in this way, then move on to the next.

When the whole piece has been waxed, buff each surface gently with a piece of soft cloth such as well-washed muttoncloth, turning frequently and making sure there are no streaks. Again, don't try to produce a high shine yet. Now leave it for several hours, preferably overnight, before the final polish. With a fresh muttoncloth, give a brisk and firm rub over. Once-over should be sufficient to produce a good mellow shine which will last for months with nothing more than an occasional gentle rub with the muttoncloth. Of course, the more you apply polishing wax the deeper the patina, but once every six months will be more than enough to maintain a good shine in normal circumstances.

Don't worry when, a day or so after applying the wax (or even after a few hours in a warm, sunny room), you find that the surface has developed a bloom. This is only a temporary effect caused by the solvents evaporating from the wax, and is easily removed by a gentle wipe with the polishing cloth.

A final point: On surfaces which would not be polished to a shine by the duster, as for example in deep carving and mouldings, or the inside top area of chair legs, apply the wax with the brush but don't rub it off entirely when buffing. Allow it to dry to a matt finish for the most natural effect, buffing with a soft brush if necessary. (For surfaces which would not be finished, but which now have an old dark colour, see chapter 12.)

15.   Wax-only finish

You might well come across a piece of furniture which has never had any other finish than wax and more wax, or has had any original finish replaced by generations of polishing. Try to avoid the use of shellac on such pieces (except perhaps *one* coat to seal in any colour). If you have a patch to disguise try to do it with water stains only—remember, though, that when working on bare wood the stain will be taken into the surface, so work with *very* thin mixtures to make sure you're in control. You obviously won't be able to conceal a glue-line by this means, except when a patch is in an area which is much-begrimed, in which case vandyke may well do the job (as described in chapter 10). Anyway, an evident repair on a piece of old oak or elm is usually accepted, so long as colour, grain, etc., are matching. (The addition of dents and marks to match those on surrounding areas is described in chapter 11.)

The basic material for building up the surface and patina is, in this case, beeswax. The first objective is to seal the surface and, if necessary, to fill the grain, and for this purpose the methods described in chapter 8 are not suitable except, of course, the wax stopping method for small areas. Grain filling on large areas is part of the bodying up process described below.

Beeswax polish

For this process you will need to prepare a soft beeswax polish. Shave a block of beeswax as finely as possible into a tin and pour on sufficient pure turpentine to just cover the flakes—about 2 oz. beeswax to 5 fluid oz. of turpentine should be right. Leave this to stand overnight, then you should have a polish which has the consistency of softened butter. If it's thin and a whitish colour you have too much turpentine in the mixture and will need to add more shaved wax, stir up and leave to blend.

Application of wax

The procedure is as follows:

  i. Rub on plenty of the beeswax polish with a cloth, working with a circular motion with plenty of pressure, until the cloth clings.

  ii. Make up a clean rubber in the same form as used for shellac polishing (chapter 6). Make sure that the wadding is very well compressed or the cover will drag; it must be really tight to do the job. Wet the outside of this rubber with meths until it feels just damp.

Burnishing with meths

  iii. Go over the beeswaxed surface with the meths rubber, again with a firm, circular motion. This will level the wax and start to burnish it. If the face of the rubber gets dirty and clogged change the position of the cover, or change it entirely if necessary. On a big job you may find it an advantage to put an outer cover over the rubber, then when you have to change it you will retain a good firm wad inside.

iv. When the surface is free of excess wax, sprinkle it with a little pumice powder (tinted with vandyke powder if open grain requires darkening) and continue with the above burnishing procedure. Keep turning the cloth on the face of the rubber and keep it just dampened with meths. *Do be careful with the application of pumice.* If it is overdone you will not only clog the rubber more frequently but the mass of abrasive which will accumulate on the rubber will soon destroy the surface you are trying to build up. Only sufficient pumice is to be applied as is required to level the wax slightly and bind that which is going into the grain. It is impossible to specify the precise quantity of pumice for a given area: suffice it to say that you should start with the finest pinch on an area of about 4 square feet, and it should be evenly distributed, so use a shaker with a very fine mesh — start with a little and you can add more if it isn't doing the job.

v. If the grain is still open, apply more beeswax with a cloth (i. above) and burnish with the meths rubber (iii. above) then leave overnight before giving it the pumice burnish described in iv.

You may have to go through this routine two or three times to build up a satisfactory depth of wax and get the grain filled. Don't rush it — let the wax dry out overnight at the stage described above, and the result will be worth the waiting. Then:

vi. When the surface is built up to your satisfaction, give it one more rub over with the meths rubber with a clean cover, followed by a gentle buffing with muttoncloth. Now leave it to dry out thoroughly; for at least two days.

vii. Since a fresh beeswax-polished surface is not resistant to marks (even the touch of a finger will show up) it will need to be protected with a hard wax finish, for which the method described in chapter 14 is ideal.

This process is doubtless the most arduous described in this book, but the deep and mellow patina it produces is comparable to the best which can be achieved by years of ordinary domestic polishing.

PART III

FINISHING — SEVERE CASES

In the preceding chapters on finishing routines we have been concerned with situations where the existing finish has been relatively sound and the surface of the wood itself of a colour which might be expected after years of exposure to sunlight and reasonable wear.

What, though, when the finish is patchy, removed by careless wear, overlain with stained varnish or other foul concoctions? And the surface itself: have stains worked their way through the finish and into that mellow outer layer in such profusion that they detract from its appearance?

Don't be put off by the physical appearance of a piece of furniture which looks ready for the tip. It it's a good piece of period furniture the lines will show through all these superficial depredations. Drastic treatment may be necessary to set it on the road to recovery, namely stripping and bleaching.

A general word of caution — don't use these techniques willy-nilly. It really is a big decision to take. To strip is to remove *all* traces of finish, right through any original finish to the bare wood. To bleach is to physically alter the surface of the wood, not just colour it. Ponder long and hard before you decide to employ them and, if you decide in favour, have several practices first on an old, varnished door or something equally worthless.

16. Stripping

If a shellac finish is too far gone to clean and revive by the methods described in chapters 5 and 6, or if it has been varnished over, particularly with that orange-red concoction so much favoured by late-19th century manufacturers and 'restorers', then it must be stripped.

Stripping off a finish is perfectly safe for even a well-faded surface if a few straightforward rules are followed.

Type of stripper

Use a thin, non-caustic, solvent-wash stripper, but not one of the viscid variety as these are too heavy to work the way this technique requires. *Stripping by means of caustic solution (soda, lye, potash) must not even be considered;* neither they nor the hot and wet method of their application are suitable for fine antique furniture — they change the colour of the wood too much, apart from the risk of damage to the surface or of opened joints and lifted veneer.

Preparation

Prepare yourself well. This is one of those procedures for which you must have everything to hand.

Make sure the piece to be stripped is standing on and surrounded on the floor by plenty of sheets of newspaper. Areas which are not to be stripped must be covered with layers of newspaper well secured with masking tape.

Have ready plenty of handy-sized pieces of rag and pieces of steel wool (3/0) — not stingy bits — good handfuls.

Plan the order in which the surfaces will be treated. Don't go about it in a random fashion and don't try to do too many surfaces at once; do large ones one at a time.

Now put on rubber gloves and some form of eye protection, preferably the safety goggles with side panels.

If you are working indoors, make sure the area is well ventilated.

Application

Decant some stripper into a handy-sized tin and apply it with a 2- or 3-inch paint brush. *Don't* leave the stripper on for a few minutes and then remove it with a paint scraper, as the instructions on the tin will probably tell you. The first can cause streaks on the surface as the stripper dries unevenly and the second may cause damage if the scraper digs in.

The most controllable and effective method of using stripper is:

Put plenty on—on a large, flat, horizontal surface (turn things on their sides and backs if you can) pour the stripper on from the small can. Don't let it stand; spread it evenly over the whole surface with the brush, *and keep it moving*. Don't let any part start to dry out; put on more stripper if it starts to. If the resulting goo builds up too much or gets so thick and heavy that you can't work it about easily, then brush it off onto the surrounding newspaper and apply more stripper.

When this action has softened and lifted all the old finish, wipe off the stripper with rag then rub over gently with 3/0 steel wool, working with the grain, to ensure that no trace of the old finish remains. Wash off with meths, finishing with a clean, dry rag, again with the grain. Allow to dry thoroughly, while you are thinking what to do next. You noticed the colour of the surface while it was damp with meths? And what visual effect do any remaining stains and blemishes have?

A good, mellow surface with attractive marks and blemishes can be finished straight away. If the overall colour is unattractive, or if the stains are excessive, then you will probably have to bleach. This decision is yours. My personal preference is to leave some minor scars and stains as long as the colour is right; they are part of the character of the piece. The colour is most important; a faded, mellow colour must be maintained, and copied on new wood used for repairs. Some pieces of mahogany furniture which have been stripped of dark varnish may be found to have an unfaded, pinkish surface. It may, of course, be left like that but usually a little help with the natural fading process will enhance its appearance.

Whatever you decide, NEVER plane, sand, scrape or otherwise remove a surface which appears to be too far gone. Consult your friendly neighbourhood restorer (see Appendix C).

Another word about stains: I am against trying to treat these individually when an overall surface is intact. Apart from the fact, as I said before, that I don't mind seeing a few marks, the treatments often recommended to remove stains seldom leave the finish undisturbed and cause a lot of frustratingly difficult work as a result. If the offending mark is only in the surface layer of the finish, as is often the case, then it might respond to some *very* gentle attention with 4/0 steel wool followed by a good waxing. Otherwise, leave well enough alone—until the day comes when, for some reason, the finish has to be removed altogether. Most stains on bare timber will respond to a solution of oxalic acid (see the next chapter for its preparation) washed off afterwards with water, but I urge you to be circumspect—if you are not exceedingly careful you can have a result which looks worse than the original stain.

17. Bleaching

Now this is a procedure which must be treated with respect and prepared for well.

Preparation You will need:

a. A two-part bleach pack (see Appendix B). This will contain two bottles, one usually marked 'A' or '1', the other 'B' or '2'. TREAT THESE WITH CAUTION, particularly the 'B' solution, which is concentrated hydrogen peroxide. Follow the label instructions for handling and storage, and always wear goggles and rubber gloves when handling.
b. A saturated solution of oxalic acid. This is prepared by adding oxalic acid crystals to half a jar of cold water, stirring well with a piece of scrap wood and adding more crystals until no more will dissolve. When you reach this stage, add a further quantity of crystals to make the proportions about ⅓ visible crystals to ⅔ water. (This solution may be topped up with water or crystals as necessary.) Again, wear rubber gloves when handling this chemical.
c. Acetic acid B.P. (33%) — half a pint will be more than sufficient for most jobs.
d. Plenty of warm water.
e. Plenty of clean rag, preferably white but certainly colourfast, torn up into handy sizes before you start.
f. Two clean jars, clearly marked A (or 1) and B (or 2) respectively.
g. *Goggles and rubber gloves.*

Application The procedure for bleaching is as follows:

i. Make sure that the area to be bleached is well stripped, grain of new wood raised and sanded, and dry. If only one surface is being treated it is advisable to screen off the rest with newspaper or plastic sheeting secured all round with masking tape. (Don't try to bleach small patches in situ — disguise them with pigments, as described in chapter 9.)

ii. Decant the 'A' and 'B' solutions into their respective jars — about half a jar of each should be sufficient for an area of five or six square feet. Follow the manufacturer's instructions about shaking the bottles. These will usually state that only 'A' ('1') is to be shaken, never 'B' ('2').

'A' solution iii. Pour on some 'A' solution and spread it with a clean piece of rag, wetting the whole area thoroughly and evenly. Keep the rag moving the whole time and never allow any part of the surface to start to dry — pour on more 'A' solution if necessary.

This stage darkens the wood — the darker it goes now, the lighter the result tends to be. Depending on the willingness of the wood to give up its colour, and the amount of colour you want to remove, the 'A' solution stage will need to be kept up for anything between 2 and 15 minutes. If you are not sure how long to give it (and you won't be until you have had lots of practice and experience), stop early and go on to the next stage. You can always bleach again later, but you can't put natural colour back in.

When you have finished with the 'A' solution, put the jar out of the way, and the rag with it.

'B'
solution

iv. Mop off any excess 'A' solution with a clean rag, then put this rag away with the 'A' jar. Before the surface starts to dry, apply the 'B' solution, spread it with a clean rag and again keep it moving and wet all over.

The time required for the 'B' solution is generally less than for 'A', usually between ⅓ and ½, but it isn't too critical. Please note that this is a departure from the label instructions, which usually state that 'B' should be left on to dry for several hours. Don't do that — the results will be unpredictable.

When the 'B' has been on for its allotted time, finish off its application with strokes which follow the figure of the wood. This will prevent streaks from appearing at the next stage.

Now that you have finished with the 'B' solution, put the jar and rags out of the way, but not close to those used for the 'A' solution — you don't want them mixed up, in case you need to use them for another application.

Note: If you are unfortunate enough to get 'B' solution on your skin, wash the area immediately with oxalic acid solution then with plenty of running water.

Oxalic
acid

v. Before the 'B' solution has started to dry, swab the surface with oxalic solution. Pour it on from the jar then spread it quickly and evenly over the whole surface with a clean rag, working with the figure.

A word of warning: If the oxalic acid starts to change the surface of the wood an unnatural colour (sometimes pink) stop, wash with warm water, dry with a clean rag and go straight to the next stage.

Acetic
acid

vi. To make completely sure that the bleaching action has been stopped, give the surface a wash with acetic acid (there's no need to wash with water between oxalic acid and acetic acid unless there has been a colour problem, as mentioned above). When the acetic acid has been wiped thoroughly all over the bleached surface, wipe off with a dry cloth, wash with warm water, dry well with another cloth then leave to dry overnight in a warm (*not* hot) atmosphere.

vii. When you have completely finished with the rags used in this process, rinse them thoroughly in a couple of changes of water before throwing them away.

viii. When the bleached surface is completely dry the colour can be checked by wiping with a clean rag moistened with meths. If it's still too fresh, go through the bleaching procedure again.

Stains

Bleaching will not only fade a surface, but will remove all but the most stubborn stains. These can be given further treatment, as described in the previous chapter, but as I said then, rather than risk spoiling the good work already done, leave well enough alone.

APPENDIX A

FURNITURE WOODS

Part I: Woods most often found in English furniture

Common name (Alternatives in brackets)	Botanical name	Chief characteristics of unfinished wood	Principal uses
Ash	Fraxinus excelsior	White, with long, usually straight, lines of grain.	18th century chairs.
Beech	Fagus sylvatica	White to pinkish-brown; distinctive fine fleck which shows as satin-brown markings on transverse cuts.	Chairs and carcase-work; gilded and painted furniture.
Birch	Betula spp.	Hard, white to pinkish-brown with fine, regular grain.	Chairs and carcase-work.
Box	Buxus sempervirens	Pale yellow, with no distinguishable grain. Works crisply, leaving a glossy surface.	Inlay, stringing and banding; fine turning.
Ebony	Diospyros spp.	Heavy and black, some with grey-green to brown stripes.	Inlay, marquetry; banding and stringing.
Elm	Ulmus procera (English) Ulmus glabra (Wych)	Light reddish-brown with distinctive figure and grain, often including conspicuous golden-brown fibres.	Chairs.
Mahogany: Cuban (Spanish)	Swietenia mahogani	Rich dark brown to plum-coloured; hard and brittle; often with white (silica) in the grain.	Second and third quarters of 18th century, in solid and veneer.
Honduras (Baywood)	Swietenia macrophylla	Paler than Cuban and lighter in weight. More open grain, again containing silica.	Mid-18th century to early-19th century, in solid and veneer

Oak	*Quercus spp.*	uniform colour, varying with species from white to dark brown. Distinguished by its grain; medullary rays prominent on end grain and quarter-sawn cuts.	century, thereafter for some carcase-work. Continued use in solid for country furniture.
Pine	*Pinus spp.*	Soft with straight figure; white to pale yellow.	Carved and gilded furniture; carcase-work.
Rosewood	*Dalbergia spp.*	Purple-brown with often highly-figured black bands and markings. Unmistakable fragrance when cut.	Veneer. Some solid work, usually turned pieces or carved detail.
Satinwood: West Indian	*Fagara flava*	Rich yellow, displaying fine, highly-reflective and variegated figure.	Veneer on fine-quality late-18th century furniture.
East Indian	*Chloroxylon swietenia*	Paler than the West Indian, and without the same depth of reflectivity.	Introduced after the West Indian; same uses.
Walnut	*Juglans regia* (European) *Juglans nigra* (American or Black)	Pale purple-brown to red-brown, with dark brown to black veining: *nigra* usually more variegated.	Predominantly from mid-17th to early-18th century, first in solid then as veneer.
Yew	*Taxus baccata*	Heaviest and hardest of the softwoods, yet extremely supple. Heartwood varies from purple-brown to orange, with thin white sapwood. Turns particularly well.	High quality chairs and small tables in the solid. Veneer.

Part II: Some other wood used in English furniture

Common name (Alternatives in brackets)	Botanical name	Chief characteristics of unfinished wood	Principal uses
Amboyna	*Pterospermum indicum* (also described by some authorities as the burr of the Padouk, *Pterocarpus dalbergioides*.	Made up of curls with many small 'bird's eye' knots, in pale brown and honey colours.	Veneers—18th century.
Apple	*Malus spp.*	Hard and white, with close, fine flecked grain markings.	Inlay, marquetry and banding.
Brazil-wood	*Caesalpinia brasilensis*	Rich red, with a grain similar to a close-grained mahogany.	17th century inlay, and again in the 19th century.
Calamander	*Diospyros quaesita*	Light brown, mottled and striped with black.	Cross-banding.
Cedar	*Cedrela odorata* (W. Indies) and other species *Juniperus virginiana* (North America)	Soft and smooth-textured with reddish to greenish-brown colour; characteristic fragrance.	Linings of drawers, presses and in solid for boxes and chests.
Cherry	*Prunus avium & spp.*	Hard and attractively figured with close grain; creamy to red-brown.	Small furniture and treen; veneer.
Chestnut, Sweet (Spanish)	*Castanea sativa*	Colour and grain very similar to oak but without medullary rays.	Chairs.
Coromandel	*Diospyros melanoxylon*	Resembles rosewood, but light stripes are pale brown	Veneer and banding.

			Linings of chests.
Cypress	*Cupresses sempervirens* (Mediterranean)	Hard, close-grained; reddish.	Linings of chests.
Holly	*Ilex aquifolium*	Extremely white; hard, with close, spotted grain.	Inlay and marquetry, sometimes stained.
Kingwood (Prince's wood)	*Dalbergia spp.*	Similar to rosewood, except that the light and dark bands are more regularly spaced.	Cross-banding.
Laburnum	*Laburnum vulgare & spp.*	Distinctive rich olive-green to brown heartwood with bright yellow sapwood—usually used together.	Oyster veneers on cabinets and desks of the late-17th century.
Lignum vitae	*Guaiacum officinale*	Dark brown to green in contrasting streaks, with yellow sapwood. Extremely hard and difficult to work.	Veneers in 17th century.
Lime	*Tilia vulgaris*	Close-grained, light and soft; white to pale yellow.	Carving.
Maple	*Acer campestris* (same genus as Sycamore (q.v.) and easily mistaken for it)	White, close-grained with shaded veining.	Veneer.
Rock Maple (Sugar Maple)	*Acer saccharum*	Produces the 'bird's eye' veneers.	Regency period veneer.
Olive	*Olea europaea*	Hard and close-grained; yellowish-green with dark blotches.	Parquetry and veneer.
Pear	*Pyrus communis*	Hard and fine-grained; cream tinged with red.	Inlay and banding. Often stained to imitate ebony.

Continued overleaf

Common name (Alternatives in brackets)	Botanical name	Chief characteristics of unfinished wood	Principal uses
Plane	*Platanus acerifolia*	Pale yellow to pale red; quarter-sawn shows lacey effect.	Gilded furniture.
Plum	*Prunus domestica*	Hard and heavy; yellow, streaked brown to red.	Inlay; turning; treen.
Purpleheart	*Peltogyne spp.*	Grey-brown when first cut, changing to bright purple on exposure to light.	Cross-banding.
Sycamore	*Acer pseudoplatanus*	Milky-white with fine, close grain.	Inlay and veneer. Stained to a grey-green colour it was known as Harewood.
Thuya	*Tetraclinis articulata*	Wavey figure in rich browns, interspersed with 'bird's eye' markings.	Veneer and inlay.
Tulipwood	*Dalbergia spp.*	Straw-coloured with pink stripes.	Cross-banding.
Zebrawood	*Pithecolobium racemiflorum*	Light brown with regular wide bands of deep brown.	Veneer and cross-banding.

APPENDIX B

LIST OF MATERIALS

List of basic materials mentioned in the text

Note: The quantities recommended should be regarded as a reasonable 'first order' stock for the home workshop making constant use of these items, bearing in mind economical order quantities and shelf lives.

Many items are still sold by Imperial measures.

Item	Quantity recommended
LIQUIDS:	
Shellac polish, very pale button or transparent	1 litre
Methylated spirit	2 litres
Turpentine — pure	1 litre
Paint stripper — solvent-wash type	1 litre
Bleach — 2-part pack, (A & B) or (1 & 2)	1 litre each
Acetic acid B.P. (33%)	1 litre
Woodworm insecticide	1 litre
Liquid soap (Teepol)	1 litre
PIGMENTS:	
Burnt Turkey Umber (dark green-brown: cool)	½ lb.
Raw Umber (pale grey-brown: cool)	½ lb.
Yellow Ochre (pale mustard-yellow: cool)	½ lb.
Raw Sienna (yellow-brown: warm)	½ lb.
Brown Umber (rich dark brown: warm)	½ lb.
Red Ochre (brick red)	½ lb.
Burnt Sienna (dark red-brown)	½ lb.
Orange Chrome (reflective orange)	½ lb.
Yellow (or Lemon) Chrome (reflective yellow)	½ lb.
Flake White (non-reflective white)	½ lb.
Titanium White (reflective white)	½ lb.
Vegetable Black (preferred to the coarser carbon black)	½ lb.
STAINS, WATER (Powder):	
Mahogany	2 oz.
Oak	2 oz.
Brown	2 oz.
Black	2 oz.
Green	1 oz.
Vandyke (crystals or substitute)	1 lb.

Item	Quantity recommended
STAINS, SPIRIT (Powder):	
Bismarck (brown)	1 oz.
Chrysoidine (red)	1 oz.
Yellow*	1 oz.
Green*	1 oz.
Black	1 oz.
*May also be water soluble	
STAIN, CHEMICAL:	
Potassium bichromate	100 grams
WAXES:	
Carnauba wax (grey)	1 lb.
Beeswax (yellow)	1 lb.
Paraffin wax	1 lb.
ABRASIVES:	
Granet paper: 150 grit (4/0), A OP ('A' weight, open coat)	Pack (50 sheets)
Garnet paper: 320 grit (9/0), A OP ('A' weight, open coat)	Pack (50 sheets)
Silicone carbide paper (Lubrisil): 320 grit (9/0)	Pack (50 sheets)
Steel wool: 3/0 (000)	2 lbs.
Steel wool: 4/0 (0000)	2 lbs.
SUNDRIES:	
Oxalic acid crystals	½ lb.
Whiting—powdered	1 lb.
Pumice powder—fine	¼ lb.
Shellac flakes	1 lb.
Scotch glue—pearl	2 lbs.
Wadding	12 yard roll
Muttoncloth	2 lbs.
Masking tape: 1″ wide	1 roll

APPENDIX C

The British Antique Dealers' Association keeps a list of qualified restorers of antique furniture (and of clocks).

For the name and address of your nearest restorer, write to:
The Secretary,
The British Antique Dealers' Association,
20, Rutland Gate,
London,
SW7 1BD.

or telephone:
01-589 4128   or   01-589 2102

INDEX

Italics indicate figure numbers